The Conflict Resolution Library

Dealing with Fighting

• Marianne Johnston •

The Rosen Publishing Group's
PowerKids Press
New York

Published in 1996 by The Rosen Publishing Group, Inc.
29 East 21st Street, New York, NY 10010

Photo Credits: Cover photo and p.12 by Maria Moreno; all other photos by Thomas Mangieri.

Book Design and Layout: Erin McKenna

First Edition

Johnston, Marianne.
    Dealing with fighting / Marianne Johnston. — 1st ed.
        p.   cm. — (The conflict resolution library)
    Includes index.
    Summary: Explains how arguments and quarrels can lead to fights and how to avoid or deflect conflict in interpersonal relations.
    ISBN 0-8239-2373-8
    1. Interpersonal conflict—Juvenile literature. 2. Fighting (Psychology)—Juvenile literature.
3. Quarreling—Juvenile literature. 4. Interpersonal confrontation—Juvenile literature. [1. Conflict (Psychology). 2. Fighting (Psychology). 3. Quarreling. 4. Interpersonal relations] I. Title.
II. Series.
BF637.I48J64   1996
303.6'9—dc20   95-50796
                                                                      CIP
                                                                       AC

Manufactured in the United States of America

Contents

How Does a Fight Start?

Sometimes we have **arguments** (AR-gyu-ments) with people. This is when we don't agree with someone about something. When people argue with each other, they try to make the other person see their side of things.

When that doesn't work, they may start to get angry. And sometimes when people get angry with each other, they start to fight.

◀ Sometimes an argument turns into a fight.

Verbal Fighting

Sometimes arguments turn into **verbal** (VER-bul) fights. Verbal fighting means fighting with words. People scream and yell at each other when they fight verbally. That doesn't do much good, since both people are so busy yelling they usually don't listen to each other. The problem doesn't get solved, and both sides become even more upset and angry.

People don't listen to each other when they are yelling in a verbal fight. ▶

Physical Fighting

A verbal fight can turn into a **physical** (FIZ-zi-cal) fight. People fight physically when they feel that words are not enough to let someone know they are upset or when they don't know how to express their feelings in words.

People sometimes hit, punch, or kick when they fight. When this happens, all hope of solving the problem is lost. The only thing that can come of this kind of fighting is that someone will get hurt.

◀ The only thing that happens in a physical fight is that someone gets hurt.

Sean and Albert

Sean and Albert were arguing about which video to watch. They became upset and started to yell at each other. Sean was so angry that he punched Albert. Albert ended up with a black eye. Both boys were forbidden to watch television for a week. The problem of which video to watch wasn't solved. Fighting only made it worse. What could they have done instead to solve their problem?

Fighting never helps solve the problem. ▶

Stop Before It Starts

Arguments are facts of life. We can't always agree with everyone. When you don't agree with someone, it's good to let that person know how you feel by talking about it. The trick is not to let a discussion turn into a fight.

The way to do this is to stay calm and listen. One person takes a turn talking while the other person listens. Then you change places. This allows you to understand each other and to solve the problem.

In a discussion, one person talks while the other person listens.

When You Feel Like Fighting

When you feel like fighting with someone, either verbally or physically, the first thing to do is calm down.

Ask yourself, "If I yell at this person, or if I hit him, will it help things or hurt things?" Chances are it will hurt things.

Both of you will be more upset and, even worse, both of you could really get hurt. And the original problem will not be fixed.

It's okay to walk away from a possible fight. ▶

Keisha and Darren

Keisha and her brother, Darren, were arguing. Keisha was so angry that she wanted to punch Darren in the nose.

But then she thought about it. Keisha knew that Darren would probably hit her back and that they both would end up hurt.

Instead, she asked Darren if they could talk about the problem later, when they had calmed down. Darren agreed.

◀ Take some time to calm down before trying to talk about a problem.

Talking, Not Fighting

Whenever you have a **conflict** (KON-flikt), or problem, with someone, the best thing to do is to talk it out. Calmly listen to what the other person says. Try to see his side of things.

When it is your turn to talk, try to say exactly what you feel. Don't be mean or hurt the other person's feelings. Help him understand your side of things. The best way to **resolve** (ree-ZOLV) a conflict is to talk it out, not fight it out.

Talking about a conflict will help solve it faster than fighting about it. ▶

Compromise

Sometimes it is not possible for you to get your way when you have a conflict with someone. If you have talked it out and you just can't agree, then it is time to **compromise** (KOM-pro-mize).

This means that both sides give up a little bit of what they want so that the conflict can be resolved.

◄ You may have to compromise on something like which game to play first.

Tina and Chris

Tina let her friend, Chris, borrow her bike. Chris accidentally broke one of the pedals.

The two friends talked about it. Tina wanted Chris to buy her a new bike. Chris didn't want to pay anything at all. So they compromised. Chris said he would buy Tina a new pedal. Tina thought that was fair and agreed.

By compromising and not fighting, the conflict was resolved.

Glossary

argument (AR-gyu-ment) Talking with someone about something you both disagree on.

compromise (KOM-pro-mize) Settling an argument by giving in a little.

conflict (KON-flikt) When two people see things differently.

physical (FIZ-zi-cal) Having to do with your body.

resolve (ree-ZOLV) Fixing a problem.

verbal (VER-bul) Using words.

Index